The Illegitimate [illegible]

A
CHRISTMAS
TWIST

by *Doug Armstrong*
Keith Cooper
& Maureen Morley

story by Doug Armstrong
Keith Cooper
Maureen Morley
& Tom Willmorth

BROADWAY PLAY PUBLISHING INC
56 E 81st St., NY NY 10028-0202
212 772-8334 fax: 212 772-8358
http://www.BroadwayPlayPubl.com

First printing: June 2000
I S B N: 0-88145-176-2

Book design: Marie Donovan
Word processing: Microsoft Word for Windows
Typographic controls: Xerox Ventura Publisher 2.0 P E
Typeface: Palatino
Copy editing: Michele Travis
Printed on recycled acid-free paper and bound in the
U S A

The Illegitimate Players Theater Company was founded in 1985 as a group of writers and actors dedicated to creating original comedies for theater and television. The company is best known for writing and producing a series of literary parodies based on the works of popular authors. This series was launched in 1989 with THE GLASS MENDACITY, based on three plays by Tennessee Williams; followed by ALL MY SPITE, based on two plays by Arthur Miller; OF GRAPES AND NUTS, based on two novels by John Steinbeck; and A CHRISTMAS TWIST, based on the writings of Charles Dickens. Most plays in the series premiered at Victory Gardens Theater in Chicago. All were taped for broadcast by T C I of Illinois cable television.

Other plays written and produced by the company include CHEESE LOUISE, a comedy set in the Wisconsin Dells; PANDORA SKULNK WON'T COME OUT OF THE HOUSE, a lighthearted look at debilitating phobias; and MYSTERY DATE, loosely based on the board game. Additional group productions include three comedy revues at the Roxy Cabaret in Chicago: NEAR NORTH SIDE STORY, OUT ON A WHIM, and THE ILLEGITIMATE PLAYERS COMEDY REVUE; and a twenty-four week television series for Group W cable of Chicago.

The company won numerous awards for its theatrical, television and cabaret productions. OF GRAPES AND NUTS received two Joseph Jefferson Citations in the categories of Writing/Adaption and Supporting actress, and two "Jeff" nominations for Ensemble and Supporting Actor. A CHRISTMAS TWIST received

"Jeff" nominations for Writing/Adaptation, Ensemble, Sound Design and Costume Design. Television awards included ACE Awards for A CHRISTMAS TWIST and NEAR NORTH SIDE STORY, ACE Award nominations for THE GLASS MENDACITY and THE ILLEGITIMATE PLAYERS ON T V,and a local Emmy Award nomination for NEAR NORTH SIDE STORY.

A CHRISTMAS TWIST was first presented by The Illegitimate Players (Producers Maureen FitzPatrick, Kathy Giblin and Sarah Steffen) on 16 November 1991 at the Victory Gardens Studio Theater in Chicago, Illinois. The cast and creative contributors were:

TINY TWIST . . . . Paul Stroili
FAGIN . . . . Tom Willmorth
MR BUMBLE . . . . Will Clinger
ANNIE . . . . Maureen Morley
EBENEZER SCROOGE . . . . Keith Cooper
BOB CRATCHIT . . . . Doug Armstrong
EMILY CRATCHIT . . . . .Maureen FitzPatrick
CAROLLERS . . . .Maureen Morley, Maureen FitzPatrick
GHOST OF JACOB MARLEY . . . . Doug Armstrong
GHOST OF CHRISTMAS PAST . . . . . .Maureen FitzPatrick
YOUNG SCROOGE . . . . Paul Stroili
MR FUZZYWIG . . . . Tom Willmorth
BELLE . . . . Maureen Morley
GHOST OF CHRISTMAS PRESENT . . . . . . Maureen Morley
GHOST OF CHRISTMAS YET TO COME . . . Tom Willmorth
GRAVEDIGGER . . . . Will Clinger
LIBBY . . . . Maureen Morley

Director . . . . .Judy O'Malley
Set design . . . . Doug Armstrong
Lighting design . . . . .Jeffrey Childs
Costume design . . . . Cheri Cory
Sound design/arrangement . . . . Galen G Ramsey
Original music . . . . David Whitehouse
Production stage manager . . . . Le'ah Razor Griffith

SYNOPSIS OF SCENES

All of the action takes place in the city of London,
Christmas Eve and Christmas Day, 1843

ACT ONE

Prologue: *Workhouse dining hall*
Scene One: FAGIN's *lair. Late afternoon*
Scene Two: SCROOGE's *counting house*
Scene Three: *The street. Early evening*
Scene Four: FAGIN's *lair*
Scene Five: *The* CRATCHIT *house*
Scene Six: SCROOGE's *bedroom. Later that evening*

ACT TWO

Scene One: *That night.* SCROOGE's *bedroom,* SCROOGE's *boyhood school,* FUZZYWIG's *warehouse,* BELLE's *home*
Scene Two: SCROOGE's *bedroom, the* CRATCHIT *house,* FAGIN's *lair*
Scene Three: SCROOGE's *bedroom, the* CRATCHIT *house, a graveyard*
Scene Four: SCROOGE's *bedroom. Christmas morning*
Scene Five: *The street. Later that morning*
Scene Six: The CRATCHIT *house.*

A NOTE ON THE CHARACTERS

FAGIN is based on the character of the same name from Dickens' *Oliver Twist*. He is filthy and conniving and leads a gang of orphan pickpockets.

MR BUMBLE, SCROOGE's nephew, is based primarily on the character of Mr Bumble from *Oliver Twist*. He is pompous and greedy and prone to coining unusual phrases and words.

TINY TWIST is a composite of Tiny Tim from *A Christmas Carol* and the title character from *Oliver Twist*. He is a lame orphan who is sent to work for FAGIN and eventually goes to live with the CRATCHITS. He is good-hearted and an object of pity, made all the more pathetic by the fact that he is in his twenties. The role is most suited to a taller actor. He should be clothed in a boy's suit that he has long outgrown and a Prince Valiant wig.

ANNIE (Little Artful Annie) is a composite of the Artful Dodger from *Oliver Twist* (With a touch of the character of Nancy from the same novel, evident in her conscience, her befriending of TWIST and her eventual punishment at the hands of FAGIN) and Little Orphan Annie from the funnies. ANNIE is FAGIN's best pickpocket. She is very smart and sly. Her appearance should reflect a Little Orphan Annie who has been on the streets for too many years: dirty, curly wig; dirty and torn blouse and jumper and a large overcoat with pockets and possibly a tattered hat.

EBENEZER SCROOGE is an old, greedy miser with no affection toward anyone, especially his clerk, BOB CRATCHIT. He has a particular dislike for the holiday of Christmas.

BOB CRATCHIT is the long-suffering clerk of SCROOGE. He is overly kind and somewhat naive.

EMILY CRATCHIT is BOB's wife and protector. She loves BOB but has a more practical outlook toward life.

MARLEY is SCROOGE's late business partner who comes to him as a ghost to warn him of his fate. He is somewhat but not overly solemn.

PAST (Ghost of Christmas Past) is a sweet but slightly inefficient old ghost.

YOUNG SCROOGE is a hard-working but happier and kinder SCROOGE. He is of marrying age when we first see him and is several years older in his second appearance.

FUZZYWIG is based on the character of Mr Fezziwig from *A Christmas Carol*, to whom SCROOGE was once apprenticed. He is an overly cheerful sort.

BELLE is YOUNG SCROOGE's fiancee. She is bright and bubbly on her first appearance but, as a result of SCROOGE's neglect, has grown cold by her second appearance.

PRESENT (Ghost of Christmas Present) is a middle-aged, loud obnoxious drunk of a ghost.

FUTURE (Ghost of Christmas Yet to Come) is a frightening ghost, fully cloaked except for a skeletal hand and an obscured skeletal face. This ghost does not speak.

Other minor characters include CAROLLERS (two Christmas carollers), GRAVEDIGGER (a cockney gravedigger) and LIBBY (an old crone), as well as a few never seen characters whose voices we hear.

The play was written so that it may be performed by a cast of seven actors, with six playing multiple roles.

A note on the play: This play, like any other, is open to a wide range of interpretation. However, it has been our experience that the script works best when played straight. As Peter Ustinov so succinctly put it, "Comedy is simply a funny way of being serious."

ACT ONE

Prologue

(A rousing symphonic overture ends on a high, tremulous note which suspends for several seconds. Over the ringing tone we hear the frail echoes of footsteps in a workhouse dining hall. They stop. Silence. A dim spot shines on TINY TWIST'*s face. He is on his knees with a bowl in his hands.)*

TWIST: Please, sir, I want some more.

BUMBLE: *(Offstage V/O)* Whaaaaaat?

TWIST: Please, sir, I want some...more. More gruel.

BUMBLE: *(V/O)* Whaaaaaat?

TWIST: *(Sigh)* I want more gruel! The runny stuff in the pot!

BUMBLE: *(V/O)* Whaaaaaat?

TWIST: *(Mumbling)* I want you to eat my shorts, you deaf old fart.

BUMBLE: *(V/O)* I heard that.

(A whipping commences, to the beat of Carol of the Bells. *Lights up on Scene One.)*

Scene One

(FAGIN's *lair*)

(FAGIN *is at a table sorting coins, jewelry, etc., into a small tin box. He is interrupted by a pounding at the door. We hear, offstage, the sounds of children scrambling for cover.*)

FAGIN: What, who's there! (*Calling to a back room*) Hide, hide, my dearies... Under the floor boards and be quick about it. (*More offstage noise. To door*) One moment! I'm in the middle of, uh...wrapping presents.

(FAGIN *hurriedly stashes his treasures, then goes to the door.*)

FAGIN: What's the password, visitor mine?

BUMBLE: (*V/O. Off*) Open the door, you filthy villain.

FAGIN: Works for me.

(FAGIN *opens the door, and* MR BUMBLE *hurriedly enters.*)

FAGIN: Mr Bumble.

BUMBLE: Ah, Mr Fagin, upon the grave of my mother, I cannot believe how long it is!

FAGIN: Why, was your mother very tall?

BUMBLE: Ah yes, I see nothing much has changed here in your filthy den of thieving pickpockets. Where are the booty grabbing imps?

FAGIN: The imps is out grabbing booty.

BUMBLE: Now, Mr Fagin, I need a favor similar to our last arrangement.

FAGIN: Mr Bumble. Whenever one of your workhouse laddies gets crushed to death in a loom you come asking for one of mine so your Uncle Scrooge won't get wind of the labor shortage. Well, my boys is not for sale, sir. I loves 'em like a family, I tells you.

BUMBLE: Last winter you gave me six for a crown.

FAGIN: So I practices tough love. But this is Christmas Eve, the biggest shoppin' day of the year. You think I'm going to give up one of my fine young assets when the purses is fat?

BUMBLE: I'm not here to buy, but to deliver.

FAGIN: Eh?

BUMBLE: I'll cut to the cranberries. I have a workhouse boy for you by the name of Tiny Twist. I would like you to take him into your tutelage. He's as fit as a ringmaster's waistcoat, has plenty of mileage left in him, been wormed.

FAGIN: Why brings him here, then? What's he done?

BUMBLE: He's too spirited for our work place. This boy seems to require an environment which will tame his wild tendencies. The Church no longer taking castrati, I immediately thought of your pickpocket enterprise.

FAGIN: I see. May I have a look at the goods?

BUMBLE: Uh...certainly. Right this way, Master Twist.

(BUMBLE *steps to the doorway and brings in* TINY TWIST. *He is in his twenties and uses a small crutch.* BUMBLE *supports him a bit.*)

BUMBLE: Don't be shy. Mr Fagin, this is Tiny Twist. Say hello, child.

TWIST: *(Looking around)* What stinks in here?

BUMBLE: *(Collaring* TWIST*)* Keep a civil tongue, boy.

TWIST: Hello, sir.

FAGIN: *(Raises arm in greeting)* Hello, boy.

(TWIST *ducks as if he were going to be slapped.*)

FAGIN: A little jumpy, isn't he?

BUMBLE: Great instincts has this boy.

FAGIN: My, he's a tall drink of tonic.

BUMBLE: Just hit his growth spurt, you know.

FAGIN: Eh, what's with the crutch? You knows I can't use damaged merchandise here, Mr Bumble.

BUMBLE: *(Taking crutch)* What, this? Merely a crafts project. *(Chucks crutch away)* And not a very good one either.

(As soon as the crutch is taken, TWIST begins to fall and BUMBLE catches him with his body, propping him up with his back.)

FAGIN: Well, I'm not too...

BUMBLE: Then it's settled. A fortuitous Christmas harvest, Mr Fagin. So long lad. *(Exits quickly)*

FAGIN: *(Runs after BUMBLE but cannot catch him and so stops in doorway and calls after him)* So that's the way it's to be, is it? Next time you needs one of my lads, I'm givin' you Boneless Mahoney. *(Comes back in. To TWIST)* Well, my dearie, I guess I'm stuck with you. Does you have any talents? I mean besides your astounding growth capacity. *(He puts TWIST on a stool.)* Has you ever stolen anything before, boy?

TWIST: I've always been told that if you steal, God will punish you by making your life miserable. *(Looks around)* I guess I must have stolen at some time.

FAGIN: Oh, that's gooood. I'm very pleased. My best dodger is an orphan like you. Little Artful Annie will show you the ropes. *(Calling)* Annie!

(ANNIE enters. She is a curly haired orphan dressed in rags. She has pupils.)

ANNIE: Yes sir, Mr Fagin!

FAGIN: Annie, meet Tiny Twist. The lad will be with us from now on. I want you to demonstrate the prowess of a pickpocket.

ANNIE: At his size, why don't he just club the buggers over the head?

FAGIN: Now, now, Annie. Strength is no match for cunning. Here, use me as an example. Look Tiny Twist, I'll put this pound note in my back pocket like this. Now watch as Annie passes me.

(They walk past one another.)

FAGIN: Did you notice anything?

TWIST: The pound note is still in your pocket.

FAGIN: Diversion, merely! What did you get, Annie?

ANNIE: *(Emptying pockets)* This bag of silver, pocket knife, your wipe, these watches, some snuff, a locket and a gold tooth.

FAGIN: *(Feels his mouth)* Give me that.

(FAGIN turns around with back facing ANNIE and TWIST. ANNIE nonchalantly reaches into FAGIN's pants and withdraws a pair of boxer shorts.)

TWIST: Hey, that's my locket. Give it back. It's the only thing I truly own.

ANNIE: *(Giving it back)* All right. You're bustin' my heart.

FAGIN: *(Turning around)* All right, boy. Here's the deal. Every day you returns with at least two pounds worth of goodies or you don't eat. Anything over five pounds, you'll get a three percent commission held in a trust fund until you're twent—uh, forty-five. Understand?

TWIST: I think so, sir.

FAGIN: You go with him, Annie. When you thinks he's catching on, let him on his own.

ANNIE: Right. *(To TWIST)* You're on your own, gimp. *(Exits)*

(TWIST hobbles out after her.)

FAGIN: Is it me or is it suddenly very drafty in here?
(Looks down and sees his boxer shorts. Picks them up)
Damn she's good!

Scene Two

(SCROOGE's counting house)

(EBENEZER SCROOGE is at his desk scribbling numbers.)

SCROOGE: ...and five, carry the two...that makes....so the train carrying the feathers would get to Chertsey first. No, no, no. That's all wrong! Cratchit!

(BOB CRATCHIT, SCROOGE's clerk, enters hurriedly. He is shaking from the cold of the office.)

CRATCHIT: Yes, Mr Scrooge.

SCROOGE: Have you finished copying those letters?

CRATCHIT: Not yet, Mr Scrooge. I believe my hand is frozen.

SCROOGE: Put it in the fire, then.

CRATCHIT: I tried, sir, but the fire has gone out.

SCROOGE: You mean it's not exciting for you anymore?

CRATCHIT: No, I mean the flames have died. It needs... *(Suspenseful music)* ...may I?

SCROOGE: Out with it, Cratchit.

CRATCHIT: *(Quickly)* May I add another piece of coal, Mr Scrooge? *(He cowers, protecting himself.)*

SCROOGE: What?! That's two this month. That makes... *(Runs to desk and scribbles)* ...on average...two a month. I suppose next you'll be wanting lamplight to write by in the late hours. The reflection of the moon off your teeth won't be good enough for you anymore.

CRATCHIT: I do tire of smiling sometimes.

SCROOGE: I doubt it. I'll get your piece of coal, but don't ask for another thing before year's end. *(He goes to hidden safe, careful not to let* CRATCHIT *see him turning the dial.)* What is my birthday?

CRATCHIT: October the twelfth, sir.

*(*SCROOGE *turns the dial.)*

SCROOGE: What is the queen's birthday?

CRATCHIT: April the fourth.

*(*SCROOGE *turns the dial.)*

CRATCHIT: Sir, I was....

SCROOGE: How many people do you need in your party for a restaurant to automatically—

CRATCHIT: *(Finishes sentence with* SCROOGE*)* add a gratuity? Eight. Sir, there was one other thing...

SCROOGE: *(Turning the dial)* If a train carrying feathers and a train carrying bricks travel from London to Chertsey at equal speeds, which will arrive first? *(He removes a small piece of coal from the safe.)*

CRATCHIT: The one that departed first.

*(*SCROOGE *slams safe and quickly reads one of the papers on his desk. Obviously,* CRATCHIT *was right.)*

SCROOGE: *(Hesitantly)* Well, what if they left at the same time?

CRATCHIT: They'd crash. There's only one line from London to Chertsey.

SCROOGE: Pick one!

CRATCHIT: Feathers?

SCROOGE: *(Smugly)* I thought you'd say that. That is why I am a counter and you are a clerk. Here is your coal. Now get back to business.

CRATCHIT: Mr Scrooge, there is one more thing. Tomorrow is Chris...

SCROOGE: You will not see the morrow if you don't return to work. Light the fire and go. I need to see a man about a horse. I expect to see you at your desk when I am finished.

(SCROOGE *exits.* CRATCHIT *goes to the fireplace and attempts to light a fire.* MRS EMILY CRATCHIT *enters.*)

EMILY: There you are.

CRATCHIT: Emily.

EMILY: Hi Bob.

CRATCHIT: Wife, what are you doing here?

EMILY: I brought your lunch.

CRATCHIT: But it's nearly six o'clock.

EMILY: The roads are slippery. It took me a while to hit something.

CRATCHIT: Emily, you've got to go.

EMILY: So the old bird stepped out, did he?

(CRATCHIT *tries to quiet her.*)

EMILY: Did you ask him about taking Christmas off?

CRATCHIT: I started to, but....

EMILY: But what? He took off and left you here to tend this meat freezer on your own. The worm. The world never saw such an evil, heartless, stale crust of a man as your old Mr Scrooge.

CRATCHIT: Emily, please.

EMILY: Dogs wouldn't lick his...

CRATCHIT: Emily, you must go. Mr Scrooge will be back any minute.

EMILY: Well, I'll not watch my dear husband freeze to his death for the likes of fifteen shillings a week. *(She goes to the safe and turns the dial.)* Have we still got the same queen?

CRATCHIT: Yes dear. Now please, you must be off!

(She turns the dial and turns again and gets the coal. She is about to throw it into the fireplace when SCROOGE enters.)

SCROOGE: Mrs Cratchit, may I ask what you are doing in my office?

EMILY: Just dropping off your Christmas present, Mr Scrooge. *(She sets the coal down on his desk.)*

SCROOGE: I am not in the habit of accepting Christmas gifts, especially those pilfered from my very office.

EMILY: How do you know it's your coal?

SCROOGE: Because it was a gift from my late partner, Jacob Marley, and is personally inscribed. *(He holds out a piece.)*

EMILY: *(Reading coal)* "Scrooge, stick this where the sun does not shine." But he's been dead these seven years. How much coal did he leave you?

SCROOGE: All that he amassed during his lifetime, plucked from the faces of snowmen. The carrots I've since eaten.

EMILY: Mr Marley was a cruel man, indeed.

SCROOGE: And handsome! But I don't have time for idle chit-chat. I have a business to run, and my business does not concern you, Mrs Cratchit.

EMILY: I'll see you at home, Bob. *(To SCROOGE)* I'll not let you dampen my spirits on this day. Merry Christmas, Mr Scrooge!

SCROOGE: Good afternoon.

EMILY: And a Happy New Year!

SCROOGE: Good afternoon!

EMILY: *(Exiting)* And a most prosperous belated Guy Fawkes Day!

SCROOGE: Cut it out!

CRATCHIT: I'm so sorry, Mr Scrooge.

EMILY: *(Poking her head around the doorway)* Be my valentine! *(She exits for good.)*

SCROOGE: Cratchit!

CRATCHIT: Yes, Mr Scrooge.

SCROOGE: I'm going to allow you to live.

CRATCHIT: Thank you, Mr Scrooge!

SCROOGE: I will also allow you to keep your situation.

CRATCHIT: *(Considers, much less enthusiastic)* Thank you, Mr Scrooge.

SCROOGE: For twelve shillings a week.

CRATCHIT: Yes, Mr Scrooge.

SCROOGE: Now get back to copying. And use your other hand!

CRATCHIT: Thank you, Mr Scrooge. *(He exits.)*

CRATCHIT V/O *(Off)* Good evening, Mr Bumble.

BUMBLE V/O *(Off)* Mr Cratchit.

(BUMBLE enters.)

BUMBLE: Salutations and greetings, my good uncle. Merry Christmas to you.

SCROOGE: Bah! *(Slaps his hand down on desk, shows the palm to BUMBLE)* Humbug. *(He flicks the bug away.)*

BUMBLE: Most antiparochial weather we're having. The snow is as thick as a widow's rump. You wanted to see me, Uncle?

SCROOGE: I've heard some disturbing reports coming from the workhouse.

BUMBLE: I don't know how those pictures got in my desk. Most owdacious, they were. A grand slander upon my name.

SCROOGE: What pictures?

BUMBLE: It's not important. Go on.

SCROOGE: I hear there's been trouble. A rapscallion.

BUMBLE: Oh no. All of our boys have close cropped hair.

SCROOGE: Not a rastafarian! A rogue! An upstart. You have a boy, I believe, who has been asking for more gruel and sending grumblings about the workhouse, inciting the other boys.

BUMBLE: Yes. A most owdacious boy. As brazen as a whore with warts. I assure you on the grave of my goldfish he will no longer be a problem.

SCROOGE: See that he isn't. I have substantial holdings in that workhouse of yours, and I can have your situation taken away if I so please. You may be my only living relative, but you are still a braying ass.

BUMBLE: I'm doing my best with the funds I have.

SCROOGE: If I had invested that money properly I could have (Runs to desk and scribbles) ...four plus the eight, carry the one...made more money in addition to that which I invested. Workhouse. Bah! Bumble, you make sure that boy causes no more trouble.

BUMBLE: I'll have the workhouse running as smooth as a goat's femur.

SCROOGE: And I'm holding you accountable.

BUMBLE: I know my business, Uncle. I've spent all of my wonder years at the workhouse. You put me there when I was but a placenta with ears.

SCROOGE: It gave you character.

BUMBLE: It gave me crabs, but I have no quarrel with that. They have a good promote-from-within policy. And I became foreman when I scarcely had a hair on my chin. So you can see, Uncle Scrooge, that I have made my most indelible mark without aid of your money.

SCROOGE: And you will continue to do so. I have no intention of dying at any time soon.

BUMBLE: You are as harsh as a gruel enema. Have I not been like a son to you?

SCROOGE: My son is dead.

BUMBLE: I know. I was there. A most unfortunate occurrence. Mother and newborn fencing the reaper with the sword of human spirit...hardly a match for a big scythe. A more gruesome sight than a leper nudist colony. Most antiparochial, believe you me.

SCROOGE: Enough! My business with you is finished. Be on your way.

BUMBLE: But of course, uncle. A most joyous noel to you...and yours.

SCROOGE: Get out!

(BUMBLE *exits.*)

BUMBLE: *(V/O. Off)* Glad tidings and mistletoe, Mr Cratchit.

CRATCHIT: *(V/O. Off)* And to you, Mr Bumble.

SCROOGE: Humbug. Cratchit! Have you completed my letters?

CRATCHIT: *(Entering with letters)* Yes, Mr Scrooge.

SCROOGE: All twenty copies?

CRATCHIT: Yes, Mr Scrooge.

SCROOGE: And enclosed a shilling in one?

CRATCHIT: The first one, yes sir.

SCROOGE: And crossed off the name at the top of the list?

CRATCHIT: The very top.

SCROOGE: Good. Send the original to the name at the top of the list and a copy to nineteen of my frien—uh—business associates—and one to yourself.

CRATCHIT: *(Smiling, although this is the worst thing that's ever happened)* Oh, thank you.

SCROOGE: And post them directly or I shall be dead within a fortnight.

CRATCHIT: Maybe you ought to post them yourself, sir. *(Hands* SCROOGE *letters)*

(Bell tolls the hour.)

SCROOGE: Closing hour. I suppose you'd like to go home.

CRATCHIT: If quite convenient, sir.

(During the remaining exchange CRATCHIT *helps* SCROOGE *into his coat, then his scarf, then his gloves, then some earmuffs, then his hat, then his boots and a muff.)*

SCROOGE: I suppose you'd also like to teach the world to sing in perfect harmony.

CRATCHIT: That would be nice, but there was one other thing.

SCROOGE: You want all day tomorrow, I suppose?

CRATCHIT: That's the one. *(He cowers and covers.)*

SCROOGE: If I were to withhold half-a-crown of your pay, you'd think yourself ill-used, I would wager.

CRATCHIT: No, no, that would be fine.

SCROOGE: What if I were to give you a really harsh Indian burn? *(He does so.)* Do you feel ill-used now?

CRATCHIT: Oh no, it's thawing out my hand quite nicely.

SCROOGE: What if I put you in a headlock? *(He does.)* How do you feel now?

CRATCHIT: As safe as a newly hatched swallow under his mother's wing.

(SCROOGE lets go.)

SCROOGE: Be here all the earlier the morning after.

CRATCHIT: Oh, I will, Mr Scrooge. Thank you and have a Merry—

(SCROOGE glares at him.)

CRATCHIT: —onette dance to your health.

(SCROOGE exits.)

Scene Three

(The street outside of SCROOGE's house)

(CAROLLER ONE and CAROLLER TWO stand at the corner, singing.)

CAROLLERS: *(To Good King Wenceslas)*
Good King Wenceslas looked out
On the feast of Stephen
When the snow la la la la
Deep and mm mm even
Brightly shone the moon that night
La la la la cruel
La la la la came in sight
La la la la Wen-ces-las

(CAROLLER ONE nudges CAROLLER TWO as CRATCHIT walks by.)

CAROLLER ONE: Please sir, a little something for the needy?

CRATCHIT: Well, I haven't much, but I certainly think I can spare a half a crown. Especially at this time of year, eh? Here you go.

(During this time, TWIST appears, sees CRATCHIT searching for coin, and waits for him.)

CRATCHIT: *(His back is to the CAROLLERS as he puts away his purse)* I think you should know, there's a crowd of people down at the next corner...

CAROLLERS: Thank you kindly, sir. *(They exit.)*

CRATCHIT: ...who are robbing carollers. So do avoid them. Now, what have I forgotten?

(TWIST sneaks up on CRATCHIT and clumsily fumbles around his pockets trying to steal something. TWIST is a horrible pickpocket.)

CRATCHIT: You! Boy!

(CRATCHIT practically saunters to him and places his hand on TWIST's shoulder. TWIST turns and tries to scramble the opposite way. He is again stopped by CRATCHIT.)

CRATCHIT: Whoa! Hold up, Speedy.

TWIST: Please, sir, I've done nothing to you. Let me on my way. *(Yells)* Somebody help me! Help! Stranger! Stranger!

(Hearing the shouts, BUMBLE enters the scene and hides to watch.)

CRATCHIT: Quiet, boy. I'm not out to harm you.

TWIST: Sir, it is but for a little food that I steal. I have nothing... no family with whom to spend this holiday. I'm an orphan. So have pity and release me, sir. Please, release me...let me go.

CRATCHIT: An orphan!? My poor boy. You're just a street urchin, picking purses for a holiday meal...how....

TWIST: Pitiful, sir?

CRATCHIT: Pathetic! You're the worst pickpocket ever! Absolutely terrible.

TWIST: This was my first attempt. I'm sorry sir. I have taken nothing from you.

CRATCHIT: *(Grabbing the boy's locket)* But what about this?

TWIST: *(Grabbing it back)* But sir, this locket belongs to me. It was me mum's. The only thing I own. The nursemaid at the workhouse said it was her dying wish that I have this locket and wear it near my heart to keep me safe.

CRATCHIT: I see. For a moment there, it looked just like my Punch and Judy decoder amulet.

TWIST: Sorry I troubled you, sir. *(He starts to walk away.)*

CRATCHIT: Wait! Where do you live, boy?

TWIST: I'm staying three streets away, in a den of thieves.

CRATCHIT: That's horrible.

TWIST: Working for a harsh, cruel man who says I must steal to earn my meals and place to sleep.

CRATCHIT: What a pity, son. I shan't let you spend another night in such a place. You know, I was shopping for a gift for my wife, but I can't think of a greater...or cheaper, gift than a darling son.

TWIST: Sir?

(BUMBLE *is aghast.*)

CRATCHIT: Would you like to come home with me, my lad?

TWIST: Would I? Oh yes, sir! Thank you, sir.

(They exit as BUMBLE *comes out of hiding.)*

BUMBLE: Bless the queen's soul. This is a most owdacious turn of events. If uncle finds out, I shall be as cooked as a turkey's hind in hell.

*(*CAROLLERS *enter again. They are dishevelled and have small bandages on their face.)*

CAROLLER TWO: They took everything. Now we have to start all over. Jesus Chr—

*(*CAROLLER ONE *sees* BUMBLE *and nudges* CAROLLER TWO. *They both sing.)*

CAROLLERS: Chr—istmas is coming, the goose is getting fat. Please put a penny in the old man's hat.

CAROLLER ONE: Sir? Something for the poor?

BUMBLE: I think not.

CAROLLER TWO: Come on, G'vnor. We know who you are.

BUMBLE: Then you'll surely know I haven't the time for you.

CAROLLERS: *(Singing)* On the first day of Christmas, my true love gave to me....

BUMBLE: Fine, fine. Here you go. *(Contributes, then exits)*

CAROLLER ONE: Quick. Let's pack some snow around a brick before he gets out of sight.

CAROLLER TWO: Forget him, look. Here comes Ebenezer Scrooge. He's rich enough.

CAROLLER ONE: 'Scuse us, Mr Scrooge. Won't you give a pittance for the poor and destitute?

SCROOGE: NO!

CAROLLER ONE: Mr Scrooge, for the cost of a glass of mead a day, we can fill a horse trough with gruel.

SCROOGE: Why would you want to?

CAROLLER TWO: With the contribution of a pound or more, you will receive a lovely spittoon. With the name of a loved one engraved on it.

SCROOGE: I insist you let me be.

CAROLLER ONE: Please, Mr Scrooge, why won't you give to the needy?

SCROOGE: Are there no prisons or workhouses?

CAROLLER TWO: Why, yes sir, there are plenty.

SCROOGE: And the treadmill and the poor law are in full vigor, then?

CAROLLER ONE: We wish not, but they are.

SCROOGE: And how is the trickle down theory doing?

CAROLLER ONE: ...The treadmill and the poor law are in full vigor, sir.

SCROOGE: Oh. I was afraid from what you said at first that something had occurred to stop them in their useful course.

CAROLLER TWO: They scarcely furnish Christian cheer, so this holiday, a few of us are endeavoring to raise a fund to buy the poor some meat and drink and warmth and drink and drink. What should I put you down for?

SCROOGE: My bad attitude? My poor posture? Take your pick.

CAROLLER ONE: But...

SCROOGE: I help support the establishments I mentioned. They cost enough, and those who are badly off must go there.

CAROLLER TWO: Many can't go there. Many would rather die.

SCROOGE: If they would rather die, then they should do it, and decrease the surplus population. *(He starts exiting.)*

CAROLLERS: *(To* Good King Wenceslas*)*
Ebenezer hoardes his loot
Just like a little squirrel
Plus he is a mean old coot...

(SCROOGE throws his hankerchief at them.)

CAROLLERS: ...who throws just like a girl.

(SCROOGE chases the CAROLLERS off stage.)

Scene Four

(FAGIN's lair)

(FAGIN is fingering his jewels; he has some necklaces around his neck as he practices his elocution.)

FAGIN: How kind of you to let me come. How kind of you to let... *(Knock at door. He scrambles to hide jewels and runs to door.)* Just a moment. *(He stashes the goods.)* What's the password, visitor mine?

BUMBLE: Crack the door, or I crack your skull!

FAGIN: *(Quickly opening door)* You has a genuine talent for passwords, Mr Bumble. May I offer you something? Tea and crumpets? Bangers and mash? Chips and dip?

BUMBLE: You may dispense with the pleasantries, Fagin. I've come about the boy.

FAGIN: What boy?

BUMBLE: Tiny Twist, the boy I entrusted to your most dubious care. The very boy I saw not ten minutes ago strolling home with Mr Bob Cratchit, the inveterate employee of my Uncle Scrooge.

FAGIN: Ah, the boy learns quick. His first day on the street, and he latches onto the most gullible sucker in all of London!

BUMBLE: I want that boy away from the Cratchits as soon as possible.

FAGIN: Why is that?

BUMBLE: My reasons are not your concern; but if you need a reason, think of what that boy knows of you and your sordid little business. It would make quite a tale for the authorities.

FAGIN: So you thinks the rat might turn pidgeon and squeal to the beak?

BUMBLE: Indubitably. And do you know what that means?

FAGIN: Yes, a beak is a magistrate, and to squeal means...

BUMBLE: *(Interrupting)* It means...impoverishment and scandal and a blindfold in your Christmas stocking.

FAGIN: I sees your point. But have no fear, for I shall send my best dodger to retrieve the boy. *(Calls off)* Annie! Come out, my dearie!

(DANNIE enters.)

FAGIN: Annie, this here's Mr Bumble, from the workhouse.

ANNIE: Charmed.

BUMBLE: Good afternoon little one.

(As BUMBLE turns away during the previous line, ANNIE holds up the ring she just took from BUMBLE's hand. FAGIN nervously snatches it from her and pockets it.)

FAGIN: Mr Bumble's discovered that instead of earning his keep on the street, our Tiny Twist has taken up with a certain family who might sing to the wrong people, if you gets my drift.

ANNIE: You ask me, it's his own fault if he got himself adopted by one of them bloody singin' families.

BUMBLE: *(Taking out paper)* Actually, it's the Cratchit family. They live in the lower flat of Number 3 Westminster-on-Surrey, Redbottom-by-the-Sea Estates. *(Hands paper to* ANNIE*)*

ANNIE: What do I care? I ain't lookin' to audition.

FAGIN: You passed some time with Tiny Twist, my dear. Wouldn't you like to bring him back home where he belongs?

ANNIE: I passed some time with head lice, too. That don't mean I'm pinin' for their swift return. What's in it for me?

FAGIN: *(Threatening)* Well, look at it this way, my dear. The sooner we gets Twist back, the less chance he has to turn us all in; which means you won't have to spend the rest of your days in Women's Prison, learning cricket the hard way.

ANNIE: Fair 'nough. I'll have 'im back before supper.

*(*ANNIE *exits.)*

FAGIN: Tiny Twist is as good as home.

BUMBLE: I only wish that were good enough. *(Looks to make sure coast is clear)* The truth is, Tiny Twist has a long history of troublemaking. I suspect that he may somehow find his way back to the Cratchits. Therefore, upon his return to these premises, he must be dealt with permanently.

FAGIN: Permanently, as in...

BUMBLE: As in dead, Mr Fagin.

FAGIN: Oh, a most unpleasant business, that. A person could land himself in a quite a lot of trouble satisfying such a request. Yes, most unpleasant.

BUMBLE: Naturally, you'll be rewarded for your efforts.

FAGIN: Unpleasant, but not unthinkable.

BUMBLE: Name your price.

FAGIN: Oh, I loves this game! Hmm, let's see...one count kidnapping, one count murder, dash of larceny...ten pounds sovereign should do it.

BUMBLE: Three pounds, and not a penny more.

FAGIN: Seven pounds, ten shillings.

BUMBLE: Three pounds sterling, and one guinea.

FAGIN: Six pounds, five crowns and four-pence.

BUMBLE: Four pounds, three crowns, tuppence and a farthing.

FAGIN: Five pounds, four crowns, three shillings, tuppence and a bingle.

(BUMBLE *gives* FAGIN *a quizzical look.*)

FAGIN: ...I made it up.

BUMBLE: Five pounds even.

FAGIN: Done.

BUMBLE: I shall obtain the money from my Uncle Scrooge, posthaste.

FAGIN: *(Shaking* BUMBLE's *hand)* Always a pleasure, Mr Bumble.

BUMBLE: You have an oozing sore on your palm, Mr Fagin.

(*He wipes his hand and leaves.* FAGIN *licks his palm.*)

Scene Five

(The CRATCHIT *house)*

*(*EMILY *is dusting or some such domestic thing.* CRATCHIT *enters.)*

CRATCHIT: I'm home, dearest wife. *(To* TWIST, *offstage)* C'mon son.

EMILY: Bob, you're late. Where's the boy?

CRATCHIT: Mrs Pickwick told you then? *(To* TWIST*)* Oops. Get up. *(To* EMILY*)* I sent her on ahead with the news.

EMILY: Only that you were bringing home an orphan boy named Tiny Twist.

CRATCHIT: An extraordinary boy. *(To* TWIST*)* Pull it out of the crack then. That's the boy. *(To* EMILY*)* He snagged his crutch in a hole in the cobblestone. A remarkable boy.

EMILY: Crutch? You brought a crippled boy home? Bob, we haven't the money.

CRATCHIT: He's hardly at all crippled, more sickly really. I carried him on my shoulder most of the way home, but he toppled off at the last corner and came up lame. But wait till you meet him. *(To* TWIST*)* Ooo, that smarts.

EMILY: Bob Cratchit, I fear you've outdone yourself this time.

CRATCHIT: You bet I have! Wife, meet our new son.

*(*TWIST *enters)*

TWIST: Pleased to make your acquaintance, mum.

EMILY: You're Tiny Twist? What is that, your name on the wrestling circuit?

TWIST: May I have a seat, mum? I feel queasy.

EMILY: Over there. Bob, may I have a word with you? Over near the andirons?

(They move to the fireplace.)

EMILY: Bob Cratchit, what has gotten into you?

CRATCHIT: I'm a daddy!

EMILY: No you are not. We cannot afford to feed and clothe a sickly, crutch-ridden gargantuan boy. We can barely survive ourselves on your paltry salary.

CRATCHIT: He won't eat much, he doesn't expend much energy. Dear, if only you had seen him in the street, frightened and alone. He tried to pick my pockets.

EMILY: Oh, a sickly, crutch-ridden, giant thief boy.

CRATCHIT: We've always wanted a son.

EMILY: Tiny Twist, may I ask how old you are?

TWIST: Twenty.

EMILY: Twenty?!

TWIST: Ish.

CRATCHIT: Twentyish, dear. You see, barely out of diapers.

TWIST: I can vouch for that, mum.

CRATCHIT: It's so much harder for the older boys to get adopted. Can't we give it a try? He's had a terrible time of it.

EMILY: All right, Bob. It is Christmas Eve, after all. And he does seem like a very nice boy. Tiny Twist can stay.

TWIST: When do we eat?

CRATCHIT: What's your hurry, son? Plenty of time for food. Merriment comes first. At the Cratchit household, we have a Christmas Eve tradition. We all tell each other our most special Christmas wish.

TWIST: Does the wish ever come true?

CRATCHIT: Certainly. Why just last year Emily wished for a son. (*To* EMILY) Dear, why don't you start?

EMILY: All right. I wish for a daughter instead.

CRATCHIT: See how it's done, Twist? All right, my turn. I wish Mr Scrooge would change his cologne. Go ahead, Son. Now you.

TWIST: I wish for a good, strong pair of legs and a healthy body, so that I can be like other boys.

CRATCHIT: No, no! Make a good wish! Like for a toy carrousel or for the queen to fall down in a puddle in front of a big group of people. Something like that.

TWIST: I wish for some food.

CRATCHIT: And that you'll get, my lad. But first, another Cratchit tradition, a rousing game of blindman's buff.

TWIST: I'm not much good at games, sir.

CRATCHIT: Nonsense. Emily, fetch me a kerchief. I'll be the blindman and I have to try to tag someone and then whomever I tag is the blindman. Doesn't that sound fun?

TWIST: It sounds pointless, sir.

(EMILY *ties blindfold on* CRATCHIT.)

CRATCHIT: Of course it's pointless. It's a game. Tie it good and tight, Emily. That's the way. Now everyone run. Here I come.

(TWIST *tries to run, but the sound of his crutch gives him away and* CRATCHIT *tags him immediately.*)

CRATCHIT: Well, you'll get better as you go on. Here, now you're the blindman. *(Ties blindfold on* TWIST*)*

TWIST: Get away, get away. Here I come.

(He tries to go after them, but as soon as he gets close they go to the other side of the stage, adlibbing various taunts and squeals of glee. Finally, after two or three tries, TWIST *stops.)*

TWIST: I feel faint.

(He collapses. CRATCHIT *and* EMILY *catch him and put him in a chair. There is a knock at the door.* CRATCHIT *answers.)*

CRATCHIT: Coming. Coming.

(Opens door, ANNIE *is standing there.)*

CRATCHIT: What can I do for you, little girl?

ANNIE: Can Tiny Twist come out and play?

CRATCHIT: Why, it must be one of your little orphan friends, Twist.

TWIST: No!

CRATCHIT: What's your name, innocent one?

ANNIE: What would you like it to be?

CRATCHIT: What's that?

ANNIE: Annie, sir. And you pegged it. I'm Twist's bestest mate. *(She has moved over to the table and lifted* CRATCHIT*'s gloves into her pocket, picks up a fork)* Is this real silver?

EMILY: That doesn't belong to you. Put it down, please.

ANNIE: There's no need to get crusty, mum. I weren't gonna give it a spit shine. There's a wonderful patch of ice in front of the church and I came by to see if Twist wanted to have a slide.

TWIST: Make her go away.

CRATCHIT: Now Twist, there will be plenty of time for our Christmas games. You may go with your little friend.

(Meanwhile, ANNIE is lifting things from around the room.)

TWIST: I don't want to go with her. She's a sewer rat.

EMILY: Twist! I agree she's not the most attractive thing, but we save talk like that until after someone has left the room.

ANNIE: *(She is next to him now.)* C'mon, Tiny Twist, don't you want your freedom?

CRATCHIT: *(Musing to himself)* Free as a bird, sliding across the ice, the wind whistling through the hole in your crutch....

TWIST: *(Quietly, to ANNIE)* I don't want your kind of freedom. And if you don't go, I'm going to tell the Cratchits all about you.

ANNIE: A snitch, eh? You got promise, mate. I like you. But be careful. Mr Fagin's got his eye on you. The good one, not the one that's all clouded over with goop.

CRATCHIT: *(Coming over)* What's all this whispering then?

TWIST: Christmas wishes, sir.

CRATCHIT: What did you wish for, Annie?

(She brushes by him.)

ANNIE: A clerk's purse, Gov'ner. A clerk's purse. *(She exits.)*

CRATCHIT: Don't be so down in the dumps, Twist. I know just the game to cheer you up. It's called "Crack the Whip."

Scene Six

(SCROOGE's *bedroom*)

(SCROOGE *enters carrying a lighted candle, which he uses to light a skimpy fire in the fireplace. He begins to change into bedclothes.*)

SCROOGE: (*Sarcastically*) A Merry Christmas, Mr Scrooge. Happy Holidays, Mr Scrooge! Have you heard the one about the Rabbi and the golf pro, Mr Scrooge? Ring in the holiday, ring in good cheer. Everyone says you throw like a girl, Mr Scrooge. Feliz Navidad, Señor Scrooge!

(*The faint ring of a bell is heard.*)

SCROOGE: What's that?... Who is it?

BUMBLE: (*V/O. Off, in a distant, shivering voice*) Scrooge...Scrooooge...

SCROOGE: (*Pause*) Humbug!

BUMBLE: (*V/O*) Scroooooge...?

SCROOGE: Hmph! Voices, indeed! I have been too long at my labor, is all.

(*As* SCROOGE *begins to turn down his bed, he hears heavy footsteps coming up the stairs.*)

SCROOGE: (*Climbing into bed*) It's humbug, I tell you! My own wearied mind is playing tricks on me. (*He blows out the candle, and a slow knock is heard. Sitting up, he re-lights the candle, puts on slippers and heads toward the door. Suddenly enlightened*) In a state of fatigue I have neglected to latch the front door properly, and now the wind has got hold of it. (*Opening door*) I will simply go downstairs and give a quick slam to the—Bumble!!

BUMBLE: *(Standing in doorway, rubbing hands together)* Lord save me, Uncle Scrooge, if it isn't colder than a Scotsman's thighs out tonight. Did you not hear me ringing?

SCROOGE: I am not accustomed to receiving visitors in the dead of night, nephew. Pray tell me what business brings you here that cannot wait until morning.

BUMBLE: I've come about the boy. The one I told you was causing trouble at the workhouse.

SCROOGE: I thought you took care of that matter.

BUMBLE: As did I, but recently he has been the cause of further outbursts. This time I fear his defiance has gone too far.

SCROOGE: Then he has had the audacity to ask for more gruel?

BUMBLE: Worse. He has asked for a bowl.

SCROOGE: The impudent little wretch. Perhaps you could apprentice the boy to a business far from the workhouse.

BUMBLE: I'm afraid not. The boy is frail and weak of mind, and therefore not suited to any line of work, save Parliament.

SCROOGE: Well, if he can't stay at the workhouse and he can't be apprenticed, what do you intend to do with him?

BUMBLE: I have already spoken with a man who has agreed to take care of the boy, for a price.

SCROOGE: Exactly how does he mean to "take care" of the boy?

BUMBLE: *(Hesitant)* He means to...to put him in such a place where he will no longer be an inconvenience.

SCROOGE: The Poorhouse?

BUMBLE: A bit below the Poorhouse, actually.

SCROOGE: The Inn of the Indigent?

BUMBLE: Below even that, uncle.

SCROOGE: Belfast Board of Tourism?

BUMBLE: *(Exasperated)* He means to put the boy in the Potter's Field.

SCROOGE: *(Taken aback)* I see. Are you certain so drastic a measure is necessary?

BUMBLE: As a substantial investor in the workhouse, uncle, you must realize that if we fail to crush this gruel insurrection immediately, it will surely lead to anarchy, and quite possibly to salad forks.

SCROOGE: I suppose there is no other choice. Very well, what is the price for...muting the boy?

BUMBLE: I wasn't quoted a price to mute him, but to kill him is five pounds. Shall I count on you to pay it?

SCROOGE: Five pounds? Hmph! I will pay three pounds and not a shilling more. To my mind, your acquaintance could put the boy in the Potter's Field with half-a-crown, if he aimed precisely.

BUMBLE: Very well then. Three pounds it is, payable upon proof of the boy's cadaveratory quietus. A good evening to you, uncle. *(He starts to exit.)* Oh, and once again may I wish you very merry—

(SCROOGE *slams the door on* BUMBLE, *whose voice immediately becomes pinched.)*

BUMBLE: —Christmas.

SCROOGE: Good evening, indeed! *(Again prepares for bed)*

MARLEY: *(Off)* Ebenezer!

SCROOGE: Bahh!

(A bell is heard ringing.)

MARLEY: Ebeneeezer!

(SCROOGE *goes to window, opens it and shouts out.*)

SCROOGE: You are wasting your time, nephew. It has been many a year since I fell for your childish games of tinkle-turn-tail.

(*He closes the window and turns to see* MARLEY's *face mysteriously appear on the door.*)

MARLEY: Aaaeeeooow!! (*Your basic wailing of the dead*)

SCROOGE: (*Turning away*) Humbug!

MARLEY: Ebenezer! Ebenezer Scrooge!

SCROOGE: Pooh pooh and double humbug!

(*Sounds of heavy chains dragging up stairs are heard.* SCROOGE *puts his fingers in his ears.*)

SCROOGE: I cannot hear you. (*He hums loudly*) Hmmhmm Nyahhhh-ahh-ahh...

(*The door swings open to reveal* MARLEY *standing in the hall. He is wearing ragged clothes and heavy chains, with strange objects attached to them [E G, trophy, bicycle horn, fuzzy dice, SeaWorld pennant]. Ominous musical stinger*)

SCROOGE: Who are you?

MARLEY: Ask me who I was.

SCROOGE: (*Shaken*) Who was you?

MARLEY: Who were you.

SCROOGE: I asked you first.

MARLEY: In life I was your partner, Jacob Marley.

SCROOGE: What does that make you in death?

MARLEY: (*Thinks for a second*) Your late partner, Jacob Marley. (*Entering*) You don't believe in me, do you?

SCROOGE: Humph! No more than I would believe in the Tooth Fairy or the Easter Bunny.

MARLEY: If that be the case, I will tell them both to scratch you off the list. Look upon me, Ebenezer. Why is it you doubt your own senses?

SCROOGE: Because a little thing affects them. A slight disorder of the stomach makes them unreliable. You may be a bit of undigested beef, a dollop of chutney or a clump of partly-chewed pork rind festering in a pool of gastrointestinal juices—

MARLEY: (Cuts him off) Where have you been eating?!

SCROOGE: The Pig 'n' Whistle.

MARLEY: You may be joining me sooner than you think.

SCROOGE: Humbug, I tell you. Humbug!

MARLEY: I know of your doubt, Ebenezer, for I was once like you. Thinking of nothing but amassing my fortune. Oh, if I had only known what little use money would be to me now! Aaaeeeooow!!

SCROOGE: What's that you say?

MARLEY: Aaaeeeooow!!

SCROOGE: No, before that.

MARLEY: I said that money is of no use to me!

SCROOGE: Mercy! Dreadful apparition, why do you punish me so?

MARLEY: As one who was naughty in life, I am condemned in death to wander through the world and witness the children I might have educated; the downtrodden I might have fed; lithesome young women preparing to bathe...

SCROOGE: You are fettered, spirit. Tell me why.

MARLEY: I wear the chain I forged in life. I made it step by step, link by link and yard by yard. The accessories I added later.

SCROOGE: Very impressive.

MARLEY: Not so impressive as the coil you yourself bear. It was full as heavy and as long as this seven years ago, and you have labored on it since. Can you tell how long it is?

SCROOGE: You know I was never good at story problems, Jacob.

MARLEY: Aaaeeeooow!! Heed my word, Ebenezer. You've still a chance to escape my fate. Soon you will be haunted by three spirits.

SCROOGE: You were always good to me Ja— *(Double take)* THREE SPIRITS?!!

MARLEY: Expect the first tomorrow when the clock strikes one. Expect the second on the following night at the same hour. The third, on the next night.

SCROOGE: Then, am I to understand that the spirits will finish with me on the twenty-seventh?

MARLEY: Yes... No. I mean— *(To himself)* Oh, I see.... Three nights, and tomorrow is Christmas... Well, no wonder this hasn't worked before. *(Addressing* SCROOGE*)* I'll tell you what. Scratch that. All three spirits will call upon you tonight, provided I can get in touch with them. Now, look to see me no more, and take heed of my condition, lest it become your own! *(With that, he exits.)*

SCROOGE: *(Climbing into bed)* I still say it's a lot of humbug!

(At this, the candle flickers out, the windows and door fly open and shut, and MARLEY *appears in the portrait over the fireplace, looking right at* SCROOGE.*)*

MARLEY: Aaaeeeooow!!!

SCROOGE: *(Burrowing under sheets)* I do believe in spooks! I do believe in spooks! I do I do I do I do I do believe in spooks!!...

(Lights fade.)

END OF ACT ONE

ACT TWO

Scene One

(SCROOGE's *bedroom*)

(*Lights up on* SCROOGE *tossing and turning in bed. As the clock chimes one, suddenly we see* PAST—*fly through the air and vanish behind the set. As she zooms by, she lets out a panicky scream. A loud crash is heard, as if she has slammed into a house. The door slowly swings open to reveal* PAST *standing unsteadily in a pool of bright light. She is wearing a long satin gown resembling a leftover bridesmaid's dress. On her head is a crown or tiara, now askew. She carries a magic wand.*)

SCROOGE: Are you the spirit whose coming was foretold to me?

PAST: (*Still in shock*) Am I?

SCROOGE: Who are you and what are you?

PAST: I am the...oh, dear me... I am, uh...ah, yes. (*Entering*) I am the Ghost of Christmas Past. Yes, that's it.

SCROOGE: Then you are the first of the three spirits summoned on my behalf.

PAST: (*After a beat*) I am?

SCROOGE: (*Flustered*) What business brings you here?

PAST: The redemption of your soul, of course.

SCROOGE: What has the past to do with the redemption of my soul?

PAST: Well, we must learn from our mistakes, mustn't we? Come now, rise and walk with me.

SCROOGE: And what if I should refuse?

PAST: Then we would proceed directly to the disembowelment.

SCROOGE: *(Jumping out of bed)* I'm coming! I'm coming!

PAST: *(Offering hand)* Bear but a touch of my hand and you shall fly on the wings of the wind.

(PAST and SCROOGE do cheap simulation of flying. Scene is transformed to the front of a frosted window, which is lighted from behind.)

SCROOGE: Good heavens! This is my old school. I was a boy in this place!

(The silhouette of a BOY appears in the window.)

PAST: It is the eve of Christmas, and yet the school is not quite deserted. A solitary child, neglected by his friends, is left there still.

SCROOGE: *(Saddened)* I know, spirit.

(A second BOY appears in the window and begins to taunt and poke at the first BOY.)

BOY 2: Year in and year out
Come Christmas eve
You have to stay here
We get to leave!
Nya nya nya nya nya!

(SCROOGE turns away.)

SCROOGE: Oh, spirit. Must I see this?

PAST: Do you find the memory of that forsaken child too painful to endure?

SCROOGE: Yes.

PAST: That boy had little family to speak of, and so became an outcast, subject to cruelty and ridicule.

SCROOGE: Yes, spirit.

PAST: Not to mention the occasional frog-in-the-pants.

SCROOGE: Yes, spirit, I know! I know!

PAST: You know because that boy was you.

SCROOGE: *(Pause)* No, spirit...The other boy was me. The one doing this... *(Pokes PAST to demonstrate)* ...nya nya nya...

PAST: I see. Well, no matter, for we have several more shadows to visit.

SCROOGE: *(Sarcastic)* I can hardly wait.

PAST: It is fun, isn't it? Now, take hold of my hand.

(She waves the wand and they fly again. This time they land at FUZZYWIG's office. YOUNG SCROOGE is at work at his desk.)

PAST: Do you know this place?

SCROOGE: Know it! Why, I was apprenticed here! It's the office of old Mr Fuzzywig, bless his heart! I should like to speak to him when he comes in.

PAST: You may speak, but he will not hear you. These are but shadows of the things that have been. They have no consciousness of us.

(FUZZYWIG enters, wearing a huge fuzzy wig.)

FUZZYWIG: Ebenezer —

YOUNG SCROOGE: Yes, Mr Fuzzywig.

FUZZYWIG: Can you tell me what is so remarkable about tomorrow?

YOUNG SCROOGE: I'm not sure what you mean, sir.

FUZZYWIG: I mean why tomorrow is a day which we treasure above all others. A day who's arrival a grown man anticipates with the innocent delight of a child.

YOUNG SCROOGE: I thought pay day was Monday, sir.

FUZZYWIG: Tomorrow is Christmas, Ebenezer!
Which makes tonight Christmas Eve, the night of The Fuzzywig Limited Annual Office Party and Luau. So be a smart fellow and finish up with those papers quickly. You wouldn't want to arrive so late as to find the guests more ripe than the pineapples.

YOUNG SCROOGE: Certainly not, Mr Fuzzywig. I shall finish directly.

FUZZYWIG: Good boy! *(He crosses and turns. He points to* PAST *and* SCROOGE *by window and shrieks.)*

SCROOGE: I thought you said he could not see us?

*(*FUZZYWIG *runs past them and leans out of window, retrieving a large bucket.)*

FUZZYWIG: The rum punch was nearly frozen. *(He exits.)*

PAST: Such a small matter to make someone happy.

SCROOGE: Small?!

PAST: Is it not? For he has spent but a few pounds of your mortal money, providing little more to his guests than a warm fire and a limbo stick.

SCROOGE: If you say his influence lay simply in a kind gesture or a grateful smile, what of it? The happiness he gave was quite as great as if it cost a fortune.

PAST: And what does that say to you?

SCROOGE: I suppose that...well, that if I were as pleasant toward my employees as Fuzzywig was to his, I could easily cut their pay in half.

PAST: *(Disappointed)* I'm not sure this is working.
(An idea) Ah, perhaps this will help.

(She waves the wand, and BELLE *comes through the office door.)*

BELLE: How's my favorite apprentice?

SCROOGE: Belle!!

YOUNG SCROOGE: *(Looking up from papers)* Merely delighted! How's my favorite girl from the wrong side of town?

BELLE: Simply enchanted!

*(*BELLE *rushes to* YOUNG SCROOGE. *They embrace.)*

YOUNG SCROOGE: In that case, perhaps you won't be needing this, after all. *(Holds up wrapped gift)*

BELLE: Oh, Ebie, don't be a tease! May I open it?

YOUNG SCROOGE: *(Holding gift out of reach)* What do you say?

BELLE: Please!

YOUNG SCROOGE: Please, what?

BELLE: Please, Mr Sausage!

YOUNG SCROOGE: That's better.

*(*YOUNG SCROOGE *hands* BELLE *the gift. She unwraps it and holds it up. It is a framed picture with the words "Scrooge Lassos the Moon" written across it.)*

BELLE: *(Reading)* "Scrooge Lassos the Moon." Oh, Ebie, it's wonderful! *(Beat)* Whatever does it mean?

YOUNG SCROOGE: It means, my dear Belle, that I do not intend to be an apprentice forever. I intend to run my own business someday; to hire my own apprentices; to pay them next to nothing and force them to sweep the soot from the chimney and the slop from the street.

BELLE: Oh, Ebenezer! You make it sound so romantic!

YOUNG SCROOGE: Dearest Belle, it is said that behind the backbone of every successful man, there lies a woman. *(Taking her hand)* Belle, will you be the woman who lies behind my back?

BELLE: *(Not really understanding but exuberant anyway)* Oh Ebie, of course I will!

(They embrace. Focus back on PAST and SCROOGE.)

PAST: But this was not to be, was it?

SCROOGE: *(Depressed)* No, spirit. There were fundamental differences between us, and she refused to compromise.

PAST: You said tomato, she said tomahto.

SCROOGE: *(Angrily)* No, I said tomahto!

(PAST looks at him doubtfully)

SCROOGE: Oh what does it matter, we were both young and poor. How were we to know what the future held for us?

PAST: For you it held great wealth, but not so for Belle. Do you remember a time when you called upon her, on the eve of Christmas several years hence?

SCROOGE: Please, spirit, must I witness every single cruel thought or action I have committed in life?

PAST: No, for I am but the Ghost of Christmas Past. For that, you would require the Ghost of Every Waking Hour Past.

(PAST waves wand. We see BELLE sitting in a chair in front of fireplace, facing upstage. She is drinking a glass of sherry. YOUNG SCROOGE stands nearby.)

BELLE: I fear your love for me is waning.

YOUNG SCROOGE: Why do you say such a thing?

BELLE: Your love letters are addressed to "Occupant."

YOUNG SCROOGE: Oh. But we made an eternal contract, a promise of our love. I had it checked out. It's legally binding even though I used a fake middle initial.

BELLE: You've changed, Ebenezer. You love money now. Money and power and those little doughy pastries that drop powdered sugar all over my upholstery.

YOUNG SCROOGE: You must understand, Belle. In this harsh world, money is the most important thing.

(BELLE *stands up, revealing herself to be nine months pregnant*)

BELLE: Is it?

YOUNG SCROOGE: Well, money and a really skilled barrister.

BELLE: (*Pouring herself another sherry*) You have no need for legal representation. I will release you from our contract.

YOUNG SCROOGE: (*Pulling out document and pen*) Please don't talk like that. Sign here please. And here. But what will become of you?

BELLE: Do not worry about me. There is always room at the workhouse for a woman with all her limbs.

YOUNG SCROOGE: Okay. See ya. (*He exits quickly*)

(BELLE *lights a cigarette, takes a deep drag, downs her sherry and exhales, holding the empty sherry glass on her stomach.*)

(*Focus back on* SCROOGE *and* PAST)

PAST: She had a large heart, yet was a delicate creature, whom a breath might have withered. Your breath often did.

SCROOGE: Show me no more, spirit! Conduct me home! Why do you delight in torturing me?

PAST: Delight? You think I delight in this? You think I enjoy spending every Christmas Eve with nasty, unpleasant people like you?

SCROOGE: But Spirit...

PAST: *(Breaking down)* You suppose I've haven't anything better to do than fly through snow and sleet with nothing to protect me but this silly little crown?

SCROOGE: I did not mean....

PAST: *(Crying)* Dashing from one rotten bit of personal history to the next, all the while knowing that I've hundreds of gifts to buy and no shopping days left!

SCROOGE: I... I'm sorry, Spirit. *(Beat)* If it means anything, I do believe I may have learned something.

PAST: *(Wiping eyes)* I certainly hope so. *(She passes through the doorway and turns to face SCROOGE.)* Goodbye, and good luck to you. *(The door slams shut, and immediately we hear the sound of fabric tearing, followed by a short gasp and the rolling crash of her falling down the stairs.)*

Scene Two

(SCROOGE's bedroom)

(SCROOGE is in bed. The bells toll the hour signaling the arrival of the second spirit, PRESENT. SCROOGE cowers under covers as he sees light shining on the other side of the door.)

PRESENT: *(V/O)* Scrooge. Yoo hoo.

SCROOGE: Leave me be.

PRESENT: *(V/O)* Open up, Scrooge. I need to use your chamber pot.

SCROOGE: Hold on.

(SCROOGE *climbs out of bed and opens door.* PRESENT *stands there, drunk and wearing a gaudy, low-cut, Christmas paper print costume and ribbons and bows dangling everywhere, very much fashioned in the barfly mode—cheap and tawdry. She carries in one hand a bottle and in the other a torch, which looks like a cornucopia but conceals a small flashlight or some other such light emitting device. The spirit holds the flashlight beneath her chin as* SCROOGE *opens the door.*)

PRESENT: Boo!

SCROOGE: Ah!

PRESENT: Ha! Ha! Ha! Soil your jammies, did ya! A mere parlor trick. Didn't your father ever do that to you when you were a boy? Hold a torch under his chin?

SCROOGE: Certainly not.

PRESENT: That's right. You had a stinky father. For the best. I knew a man burned off his face doing that trick. (*She laughs loudly, then looks at* SCROOGE *who is not laughing.*) I guess you had to be there.

SCROOGE: You are the second spirit sent to enlighten me, are you not?

PRESENT: (*Trying to pull herself together*) I am the Ghost of Christmas Present. Look upon me!

SCROOGE: I'd rather not.

PRESENT: What's the matter? Am I not rich enough? (*Threatening*) Am I not rough enough? (*She falters, a little nauseated*)

SCROOGE: (*Pointing to bed*) Chamber pot's under there.

PRESENT: I'm all right now.

SCROOGE: Spirit, you appear to be a little more spirited than most.

PRESENT: It's Christmas!

SCROOGE: Humbug.

PRESENT: What!? You don't believe in the spirit of Christmas? Have you never seen the like of me before?

SCROOGE: Once or twice on leave in my Royal Navy days.

PRESENT: Look, do you want to learn your lesson or not? I've got parties to go to.

SCROOGE: Conduct me where you will and let me profit by it—if you have aught to teach me other than how to spell my name in the snow. How do we travel?

PRESENT: Pull my finger.

SCROOGE: You can't fool me, Spirit. That one my father did do. Shall I hold onto your robe then?

PRESENT: No, you must close your eyes, stand on one foot, and hop in a circle while saying "Scrooge uses huge screws," quickly three times.

(SCROOGE *does this. When he has finished...*)

SCROOGE: Are we transported, yet still in my empty bedchamber? Is this what you wanted me to see?

PRESENT: No, that's what I wanted to see. You are a stupid man, Ebenezer Scrooge. Come, we can walk from here. I know a good pub on the way. *(Exiting)* Have you heard the one about the rabbi and the golf pro?

SCROOGE: Yes!

(*Lights up on the* CRATCHIT *house.* CRATCHIT *enters and* TWIST *hobbles behind.* SCROOGE *and* PRESENT *look on.*)

CRATCHIT: *(Somewhat out of breath)* Oh, I daresay that was the best Christmas punt, pass and kick competition the Cratchits have had in a long time. I don't know about you, Twist, but I've certainly worked up an appetite.

(TWIST *falls onto the floor.* CRATCHIT *helps him to his stool at the table.*)

CRATCHIT: Up you go.

TWIST: Will Mrs Cratchit be back from the baker soon?

CRATCHIT: Oh, very soon. And with her, our Christmas feast!

TWIST: I've often dreamed about a real family Christmas. Although my mind blocked out the athletics part. But I dreamt of a roaring fire and stockings hanging by the mantle brimming with sweets, and presents, lots and lots of presents.

CRATCHIT: Heh, heh. What dreams you have, boy!

TWIST: Will there be a goose?

CRATCHIT: Not exactly a goose. But you should see the amazing things the baker can do with some shoe leather and a piece of celery.

TWIST: Shoe leather?

CRATCHIT: Not today, my boy. Not on Christmas!

TWIST: Please, don't mess with my head like that, sir.

CRATCHIT: On Christmas we have gruel!

TWIST: Gruel, sir?

CRATCHIT: Gruel and a lovely green bean and french fried onion casserole.

TWIST: You are joking again, aren't you, sir?

CRATCHIT: Don't fear, Tiny Twist, I'm quite in earnest. Wipe that tear from you eye.

TWIST: (*Catching on and not happy about it*) You're poor, aren't you?

CRATCHIT: No one is poor on Christmas, son. We are rich in spirit and love for our fellow man.

TWIST: Don't avoid the question. You're a bleedin' pauper. You don't have bob to your name.

CRATCHIT: I certainly do. One Bob. Bob Cratchit. Heh, heh.

TWIST: I'm not even going to humor you anymore. Revive me when the gruel wagon gets here.
(Head collapses on table)

(EMILY Cratchit enters carrying a couple of pots.)

EMILY: Ow! Ah! Oh! Ow! Hot, hot hot! Ah!
(She drops the pots on the table.)

CRATCHIT: Hello, wife.

EMILY: Is everyone ready for Christmas dinner?

TWIST: We don't have to have any more merriment first, do we?

CRATCHIT: Plenty of time for more games later, Twist. Dish out the feast, my dear.

(They eat while focus shifts to SCROOGE and PRESENT. PRESENT waves her light at the CRATCHIT scene.)

SCROOGE: Is there a peculiar flavor in what you sprinkle from your torch?

PRESENT: There is. It is the flavor of Christmas cheer. Tastes like chicken.

(Focus shifts back to CRATCHITS, who are just finishing up.)

EMILY: Did you want some more gruel, Tiny Twist?

TWIST: *(Cowering)* No, no, I don't want some more gruel. I'm full to the ears. Don't hurt me.

EMILY: Well, I'll fry the rest up for breakfast then.
(She clears plates)

CRATCHIT: Nothing like waking up to a hot, steaming gruel patty in the morning is there, Twist?

TWIST: *(Matter-of-fact)* You're insane.

CRATCHIT: *(To* EMILY*)* Fetch in the pudding, my love.

(EMILY *exits to kitchen)*

TWIST: There's pudding?

CRATCHIT: The finest in all the land. A rare and wonderful pudding. Why, just the other day, a man in the street said he would pay a half a pound for a taste of my wife's pudding.

EMILY: *(V/O)* You misheard, dear.

CRATCHIT: Nevertheless, it's a credit to the whippy dessert family.

TWIST: My tongue is near down to my knees!

CRATCHIT: *(Teasingly)* I do hope the pudding's still there. I do hope no one's stolen it.

TWIST: That would be the kicker.

(EMILY *enters with the pudding.)*

EMILY: Here, we are.

CRATCHIT: I think this is your greatest success.

(TWIST *reaches for pudding.)*

EMILY: None for you, Tiny Twist. I poured a full quartern of brandy on top and you're underage.

CRATCHIT: Let him have a little bit for the toast, dear.

EMILY: *(To* TWIST*)* All right, but you mustn't eat any.

(CRATCHIT, EMILY *and* TWIST *each grab a handful of pudding and hold it up, toast fashion.)*

CRATCHIT: *(Toasting)* A Merry Christmas to us all!

EMILY *&* TWIST: Merry Christmas!

(EMILY *and* CRATCHIT *eat some of their pudding.* TWIST *throws his back.* CRATCHIT *goes to toast again.* TWIST *has to grab more pudding.)*

CRATCHIT: And a Merry Christmas to other people besides us!

EMILY & TWIST: *(Monotone and out of sync)* Merry Christmas to other people besides us.

(EMILY and CRATCHIT eat again.)

CRATCHIT: *(Toasting again)* I give you Mr Scrooge!

EMILY: Mr Scrooge! I'll not toast to that crusty tightwad. That hawk-nosed monster. That pimple-necked, hairy-backed troll.

SCROOGE: *(To PRESENT)* Shut her up. Wave that thing at her and shut her up.

CRATCHIT: But dear, it's Christmas.

EMILY: Why not toast Bloody Mary while we're at it or Henry the Eighth? Here's to taxation! Let's hear it for tight undergarments!

CRATCHIT: Now you've got the Christmas spirit. Oh, look, dear. Just one bit of pudding left. Shall we? *(He glances at TWIST.)*

(TWIST looks at the pudding eagerly. EMILY nods to CRATCHIT. CRATCHIT grabs it and runs.)

CRATCHIT: Keep away from Twist! *(He runs from room)*

TWIST: I don't much like the Cratchit family traditions.

(He runs after, as does EMILY who returns with the pudding and keeps running from TWIST. She and CRATCHIT toss pudding back and forth. Focus back on SCROOGE and PRESENT)

SCROOGE: Spirit, tell me if Tiny Twist will live.

PRESENT: I see a vacant seat, a crutch without an owner, a long, drawn-out civil suit...

SCROOGE: *(Thinks)* Spirit, tell me if Tiny Twist will live.

PRESENT: If the shadows I describe remain unaltered by the future, the child will die.

SCROOGE: He's to be killed by a chair and a crutch?

PRESENT: It's imagery, Scrooge. I'm getting a headache.

SCROOGE: No! No! *(Present grabs her head)* Say he will be spared! *(He shakes her)*

PRESENT: Just for that, no. You said yourself if he be like to die, he had better do it and decrease the surplus population.

SCROOGE: What, do you spooks take notes?

PRESENT: Come, we have another destination.

SCROOGE: Just a while longer here, Spirit.

PRESENT: I'm not paid by the hour, Scrooge, and I'd just as soon dump you as save you, so get a move on.

(Lights up on FAGIN's lair. FAGIN and BUMBLE are drinking from mugs.)

BUMBLE: You will get your price when I have proof that you have taken care of the boy. The locket that he wears around his neck.

BUMBLE: When do you plan to execute the owdacious deed, Mr Fagin?

FAGIN: This very night.

SCROOGE: I recognize my nephew but who is the other man?

PRESENT: You with cheaper socks.

SCROOGE: You think I look like him?

PRESENT: It's imagery! Be still and listen.

BUMBLE: Have you devised a means of removing the boy from his planetary obligation, a method for his deceasement?

FAGIN: Upon the queen's belly, I wish you'd speak like a human.

BUMBLE: My speech is as clear as an albino's spittle.

PRESENT: I can't understand a word either of them is saying.

SCROOGE: Nor I. I hope my life does not hinge on this particular lesson.

FAGIN: I have concocted several possible alternatives for the boy's demise. I thought first to runs him over with a coach. Too chancy.

BUMBLE: Indeedy.

FAGIN: Then I thought to thrust a bag over his head and dump him in the river.

BUMBLE: Too risky?

FAGIN: No, the river is frozen. So I concocted a plan so cruel, so brutal even I wouldn't thinks of carrying it out.

BUMBLE: And what's that?

FAGIN: I told you. I'm not going to do it.

BUMBLE: Oh. What's left?

FAGIN: I'm going to shoot him in the head.

BUMBLE: Very practical.

FAGIN: Then I will bend him into a pretzel and roll him in a ring of salt as a lesson to any other boys who may entertain notions of leaving my little social club.

BUMBLE: I leave you to your ill-deed, Mr Fagin. Thanks for the cocoa.

(BUMBLE *exits. A sound is heard outside.*)

FAGIN: Who goes there?

BUMBLE: *(V/O)* Pay no heed. I just tripped over your poodle.

FAGIN: I doesn't have a poodle. *(He rushes out.)*
You little scalawag! I'll teach you to spy on me!

(FAGIN appears silhouette in window along with ANNIE.
As the all-important ominous music wells up, he grabs her
and slaps her around.)

SCROOGE: *(Totally oblivious to the action in the window)*
Oh, spirit. I'm beginning to see my ignorance, my
disregard for human life. Is a spirit's life thus short?

PRESENT: When you put away the sauce like I do it is.

FAGIN: *(He shakes ANNIE and we hear something drop from*
her pocket.) What's this? You've been holding out on me.
What else has you got? I'm going to have to teach you a
lesson, you spying, traitorous little moptop. *(He drags*
ANNIE *away from the window.)*

SCROOGE: Spirit, forgive me for asking but I see
something strange and not your own protruding
from your skirts.

PRESENT: You keep Christmas your way, I'll keep it
mine. Oh, what the hell, I'll be dead in a couple of
hours. Take a peek.

(The spirit throws open her robe to reveal an incredibly
emaciated and lifelike boy and girl.)

SCROOGE: Spirit, are they yours?

PRESENT: They are Man's. And they cling to me because
of the powerful static in my robe. This boy is Ignorance.
This girl is Want. The girl wants Ignorance, and
Ignorance is too stupid to want the girl. Beware the
boy most, for on his brow I see that written which
is "Doom," unless the writing be erased.

SCROOGE: Have they no refuge or resource?

PRESENT: Are there no prisons? Are there no
workhouses? Are there no paper routes? But who
will hire them without experience, and how can they

get experience if no one will hire them. *(The bell tolls the hour.)* It's an ugly world, Scrooge, I'm glad I'm leaving.

(Spirit exits)

SCROOGE: Spirit, wait! *(Counts on his fingers)* Past, present...uh-oh.

Scene Three

(SCROOGE's bedroom)

(SCROOGE on his knees, nervously looks upward to speak.)

SCROOGE: Oh heavenly spectre, hear me now, I am no longer the man I was. If you choose to forfeit this last visitation, I assure you I will mend my wayward means. *(The bell tolls)* Can this be so?... Spectre?... Marley?... *(Hearing nothing)* Yes! Okay, then. I'm a new man, yessiree! Thank you, spirits, thank you.

(Dramatic musical stinger as door flies open. In the doorway stands FUTURE, seven feet tall in a hooded black cloak. As he enters the room, he steps off of a small box previuosly hidden by his cloak. He approaches SCROOGE, sensing something is wrong. Looking back, he hurries to the door, retrieves the box and places it near SCROOGE to stand on. As he steps up, SCROOGE is again startled.)

SCROOGE: Oh! *(Gasp)* I am in the presence of...you're the Ghost.... Oh which Ghost of Christmas are you?

(FUTURE does not answer, but points downward with his hand.)

SCROOGE: What? You're the Ghost of Christmas Downstairs? Are my slippers on backwards?

(FUTURE starts to charade, first mimicking a flute, then a chair.)

SCROOGE: Two syllables, first syllable, arrow in cheek? Flute? Yes? I must say, charades has always been my game. Second syllable, toboggan? Rosebud? Chair? Chair!? Flute, chair, flute, chair...Future? The Ghost of Christmas Future. I'm so glad you didn't do Ghost of Christmas Yet to Come. But will you not speak to me?

(No reply. FUTURE points forward.)

SCROOGE: All right. Lead on, then. Lead on! The night is waning fast.

(FUTURE starts toward the door.)

SCROOGE: Can you not make a sound, or is this your choice of communication?

(FUTURE turns to him but does not speak.)

SCROOGE: Okay, okay, I'm sorry, lead on. This time is precious to me.

(FUTURE again starts through the door.)

SCROOGE: How should I address you?

(FUTURE spins toward SCROOGE, obviously agitated by the interruptions.)

SCROOGE: I know, I know, Sorry. Please, continue, I'm ready. After you, Stretch. *(They exit.)*

(Lights up on the CRATCHIT house. EMILY stokes the fireplace. SCROOGE and FUTURE appear on the side. CRATCHIT slowly enters.)

EMILY: You're late, Bob. Your dinner is cold and has hardened into a curling disc.

CRATCHIT: It does not matter, Emily. I'm sorry I'm late, but it seems I'm walking a little slower now.

EMILY: When you brought Tiny Twist home upon your shoulders, you walked very fast indeed. He was so very light to carry.

CRATCHIT: Again today, I carried Tiny Twist on my shoulders, and again he was very light to carry...it was the big pine box that slowed me down.

EMILY: Poor Tiny Twist. A fatal wound to the head...

CRATCHIT: ...his limbs secured like a pretzel, and placed inside a giant ring of salt.

EMILY: Poor boy. And so close to Christmas.

SCROOGE: The boy is dead? Am I to blame for this? There must have been some terrible mistake. You can't get that kind of assault for only three pounds.

(FUTURE *throws up his arms in exasperation.*)

SCROOGE: What!? What did I say?

(*Lights up on a graveyard. A* GRAVEDIGGER *kneels by two grave stones, resting a shovel on his shoulder and holding a skull in one hand.*)

GRAVEDIGGER: *(To skull)* Sorry 'bout this, Clarence. If it were up to me, I'd of buried 'im in the stables. Or right in the middle of the road, maybe the same spot where you got run over, heh, heh. (*Mimicking skull talking) Bugger off. (Slapping skull)* 'Ey watch it. You know, Clarence, you were just about the most annoying man I ever met, but even you weren't as despised as this reprobate. *Piss off.* Kiss me! Kiss me on the lips, you cheeky bastard.

(*He does as* TWIST *enters)*)

GRAVEDIGGER: Ah, there you are, Libby. Everyone else 'as come an' gone. Ain't nothin' left but the minister's spit on the coffin.

LIBBY: Tha's all right. Don't much care for pickin' over someone once 'e's been planted. Strips 'em of 'is dignity. Besides, the light's better in the bedchamber. 'Ere, undo me bundle.

GRAVEDIGGER: Libby, you were born to make your fortune. *(Peering into bag)* What is this 'ere?

LIBBY: 'Is muslin bedsheets.

GRAVEDIGGER: Libby, you didn't steal these sheets out from under 'im did you?!

LIBBY: 'Course not. They was hanging outside.

GRAVEDIGGER: Goodness. The thought of takin' 'is bedsheets while he lies there dead n' cold gives me the willy's. What's this?

LIBBY: The pants he died in.

GRAVEDIGGER: *(Dropping the bag)* Ughhh!

LIBBY: Tried to get 'is shirt too, but 'is arms were stickin' straight out like this. *(She puts her arms out.)*

GRAVEDIGGER: That's enough.

LIBBY: I looked for somethin' to pry 'em back down with...

GRAVEDIGGER: Enough!

LIBBY: Oh, pull yourself together. 'Ee was a foul sort to be sure. I say good riddance to 'im.

GRAVEDIGGER: 'At's why I left the box open a crack an' put 'im in a spot 'at's good an' wormy. All right, I'll give you four quid if you bring it to me buggy.

LIBBY: Fair 'nough, Gov'na.

(They exit.)

SCROOGE: Good Lord, the man they speak of must have been a hellish monster. A rotten, selfish ingrate who had no regard for others around him. *(Realizing it may be himself)* Nice sheets though. Are we quite done here?

(FUTURE points toward grave stone.)

SCROOGE: *(Suddenly frightened)* Ooo, I could not. I haven't the strength.

(FUTURE *gives* SCROOGE *a quick but sharp shove toward the grave stone.*)

SCROOGE: (*Carefully walking toward the stone then stopping to the side of it looking past*)
Here lies the body of Clarence Tate
Murdered before his time
Though his chosen art led to his fate
He loved the life of a mime.

(FUTURE *slaps back of* SCROOGE's *head which forces it down to stone.* SCROOGE *reels toward* FUTURE *before he reads it.*)

SCROOGE: Before I examine this stone, Spirit, answer me one question. Are these the shadows of the things that will be, or that might be if the things that be were different?

(FUTURE *is confused*)

SCROOGE: I mean, if the shadows of the things that be had not been, would the foreshadowed shadows be overshadowed by the things that will be, based on the things that will not have been?

(FUTURE *is very confused*)

SCROOGE: Just tell me, Spirit, is you is or is you ain't my future?!

(*With yet another ominous musical stinger,* FUTURE *points* SCROOGE *to the proper grave stone.*)

SCROOGE: (*Slowly looks at stone*) Oh no! It's me! Ebenezer—Aaron—Scrooge... They spelled my middle name wrong. No no. Spirit! (*On knees clutching robe*) Hear me! I am not the man I was. I will honor Christmas in my heart, and will try to keep it all year. Tell me I may sponge away the name on the stone... and get my pants back.

(FUTURE *steps toward exit.* SCROOGE *scrambles to him and grabs his shoulders.*)

SCROOGE: Spirit, assure me that I yet may change the shadows you have shown me by an altered life.

(*While* SCROOGE *holds* FUTURE's *cloak, the actor slips out of it and through an exit, unseen by the audience. The cloak drops to the ground.* SCROOGE *vainly tries to sift through it.*)

Scene Four

(SCROOGE's *bedroom*)

(SCROOGE *is wrestling with the blanket. He awakens, sits up and peers over the bed. He pats himself down to make sure he's still alive, and is overcome by glee.*)

SCROOGE: Am I alive? Am I all here? (*Pats himself down*) Oh, yes! I'm alive! I'm alive! Whoop! Look, I can jump up and down and kick my heels, and pat my head and rub my tummy at the same time. Well, what difference does it make if I can't do that? I'm alive! And I'm a new man. Thank you, Spirits! (*Grabs purse and runs to window*) Hee, hee, hee, hee, hee. (*Throws open window*) Boy, hey you, boy!

BOY: (*V/O*) Me, sir?

SCROOGE: An intelligent boy. A remarkable boy! Yes, you. What day is it, my fine fellow?

BOY: (*V/O*) Why, Christmas Day, Sir.

SCROOGE: I haven't missed it. My lad, I need a big Christmas goose.

BOY: (*V/O*) Mommy!

SCROOGE: Boy, wait! (*Searching purse*) I've got a guinea up here.

BOY: (*V/O*) I'm getting the constable!

SCROOGE: No. Here. (*Tosses down coin*)

BOY: (*V/O*) Ow!

SCROOGE: I need you to hurry down to the Poulterer's and buy the prize goose in the window. Not the little, scrawny prize goose, the big one.

BOY: *(V/O)* What, the one as big as me?

SCROOGE: That's imagery. Hee, hee. What an amazing young man. Yes, my buck. Come back with it in less than five minutes, and there will be half-a-crown for you.

BOY: *(V/O. Exasperated)* It's as big as me, sir.

SCROOGE: Oh right. *(Scribbles on paper)* Well, have the poulterer take it to this address. *(Tosses out paper)* Merry Christmas, my little man. *(Tosses out coin)*

BOY: *(V/O)* Merry Christmas, sir! Thank you, sir! You throw like a girl, sir!

SCROOGE: *(Closes window)* Hee, hee. Whoop! *(He dances around.)* I am as light as a feather, as merry as a schoolboy. I feel pretty and giddy and bright!

(BUMBLE enters. SCROOGE's arms are outstretched and BUMBLE drops locket in his hand.)

BUMBLE: Are you feeling well, Uncle?

SCROOGE: Merry Christmas, nephew. What's this?

BUMBLE: The boy's locket. Proof of his disenanimation. He shan't be a threat any longer.

SCROOGE: I am too late. Oh, cruel spirits. Why punish me thus? Why have I been spared and the boy taken?

BUMBLE: Because you're rich and have powerful connections and the boy was a lame pauper.

SCROOGE: Leave me! I must go to the Cratchits and beg their mercy.

BUMBLE: The little matter of remuneration for services rendered.

SCROOGE: You shall have it in hell. Now leave my presence.

BUMBLE: We said we weren't going to exchange this year.

SCROOGE: Get out! And don't bother returning to the workhouse. I intend to see that your situation is revoked. And that foul partner of yours will swing from the hangman's noose for his doings.

BUMBLE: *(Exiting)* Most antiparochial!

SCROOGE: *(Yelling after him)* I never understood that! *(To himself)* It shan't be a Merry Christmas after all.

(SCROOGE exits.)

Scene Five

(The Street)

(BUMBLE is hurrying down the street, rather distraught. FAGIN appears.)

FAGIN: Rather a brisk morning for a walk, isn't it, Mr Bumble?

BUMBLE: *(Looking around)* Mr Fagin, it is most unprudent to be seen at this juncture.

FAGIN: Blast it! Nobody talks like that! Speak like a normal man. Answer me, where's my money?

BUMBLE: My Uncle Scrooge would not pay the sum. He would have you hanged for your doings, and he is stripping me of my position at the workhouse.

FAGIN: He seems to like you better than me.

BUMBLE: You speak glibly for a man in the shadow of the hangman's noose.

FAGIN: It's a flaw in my character. I doesn't work and play well in groups neither. You forget, Mr Bumble, that this plan was your inspiration.

BUMBLE: But I did not carry it out. You have no proof.

FAGIN: Proof is easy enough conjured up. We had an agreement. I wants my five pounds.

BUMBLE: Impossible. I've fallen from my uncle's favor. He'll never give me the money.

FAGIN: But you are in the will.

BUMBLE: He'll have me struck out of the will to be sure.

FAGIN: Can't be done, Mr Bumble. Not on a holiday, not on Christmas.

BUMBLE: What are you saying?

FAGIN: I'm sayin' strike while the iron is hot. Get my five pounds. Deal with your uncle permanently. *(Takes out knife)*

BUMBLE: Permanently, as in...?

FAGIN: *(Frustrated)* As in dead, Mr Bumble!

BUMBLE: But I could not....

FAGIN: Scrooge has ruined you, humiliated you— not paid my five pounds—castrated you, made you look like a complete fool.

BUMBLE: *(Grabs knife)* I shall send him on a one-way coach to the Elysian Fields.

FAGIN: Not too scary but nicely put.

BUMBLE: If you want your money, you must assist me. Better yet, I will assist you. *(Skittishly hands knife to* FAGIN*)*

FAGIN: What will you do?

BUMBLE: Choreograph the plan of attack. Come, we will find him at the Cratchits. *(Exits)*

FAGIN: The Cratchits, you say? Mr Bumble, wait!

Scene Six

(The CRATCHIT house)

(CRATCHIT and EMILY stand over the incredibly large prop goose on the table.)

EMILY: Oh, Bob I've never seen such a goose! Who could have sent it?

CRATCHIT: Here's a note. *(Reads)* Have authorized poulterer to send a goose of up to twenty-five stones. Hee haw and Merry Christmas. Ebenezer Scrooge.

EMILY: *(Puts ear to goose)* It's not ticking. Has he gone daft?

CRATCHIT: Quite likely. We better cook it before he comes to his senses. But we must show it to Twist. Where is he?

EMILY: I haven't seen him all morning.

CRATCHIT: His crutch might be caught in the floor boards again. I'll give a peek.

(A knock at the door. CRATCHIT stops. EMILY looks out window.)

EMILY: It's Mr Scrooge.

CRATCHIT: Hide! *(He grabs the goose.)*

EMILY: I can't. He's seen me.

(CRATCHIT goes to door and opens it.)

CRATCHIT: Mr Scrooge.

SCROOGE: Cratchit, I've done something terribly wrong.

CRATCHIT: Yes, we know. *(Tosses him goose)* Here you are.

(He tries to close the door but SCROOGE *maneuvers goose so it's neck gets caught in door.* SCROOGE *comes in.)*

SCROOGE: No. That's for you. Merry Christmas.

CRATCHIT: *(Taking goose and putting it back on table)* Thank you, Mr Scrooge.

SCROOGE: No, the terrible thing I did was having your son killed and rolled into a dead pretzel thing.

CRATCHIT: *(Stunned)* You mean...Twist?

SCROOGE: Twist, rolled...what does it matter? He's dead.

EMILY: How awful. Has this goose been stuffed?

SCROOGE: I intend to make it up to you, Cratchit. I am a rich man. I can offer you ample compensation.

CRATCHIT: Money cannot mend a broken heart.

EMILY: It's a start, Bob.

CRATCHIT: *(Starting to like the idea)* I do need a new pair of gloves without fingers.

EMILY: And a new house!

CRATCHIT: And some polish for my boots.

EMILY: An emerald brooch.

CRATCHIT: And a pair of mink hunting socks!

EMILY: It's a dream come true!

(TWIST enters.)

TWIST: Merry Christmas, everyone!

SCROOGE: Twist! You're alive! *(He runs over and hugs him.)*

CRATCHIT: *(Sullen)* Merry Christmas.

EMILY: *(Sullen)* Oh piss.

TWIST: *(Still being hugged)* Who is this?

SCROOGE: *(Giddy again)* I'm your Uncle Ebie-Nebby. Hee hee. We thought you were dead, my boy.

TWIST: I noticed nobody bothered checking. My leg has been caught in a loose bedspring for hours.

SCROOGE: *(Pulling out locket)* If you are alive, I wonder who this could belong to.

TWIST: My locket!

SCROOGE: So it is yours. *(Gives it to TWIST)*

TWIST: It's my most treasured possession. It was me mum's. Little artful Annie nicked it from me when he *(Points at CRATCHIT)* let her in the house last night.

SCROOGE: Well, she just may have saved your life, my lad.

CRATCHIT: Look what Mr Scrooge brought for us, Twist.

TWIST: A goose! *(Looks at the CRATCHIT suspiciously)* What's the catch?

SCROOGE: No catch. It's just my way of saying Merry Christmas.

TWIST: I don't know how to thank you, Mr Scrooge. These people say it with gruel patties.

SCROOGE: Not anymore. Cratchit, my boy, I'm giving you a raise. From now on, you'll make fifteen shillings a week.

CRATCHIT: That's what I made before.

SCROOGE: No, I lowered it to twelve, remember?

CRATCHIT: Yes, sir.

SCROOGE: And I'm not going to send you any more chain letters.

CRATCHIT: Oh, thank you! Thank you, Mr Scrooge! I just wish we had something to give you in return.

TWIST: I'd like you to have this, Mr Scrooge.
(*Offers him locket*)

SCROOGE: Oh no, I couldn't....

TWIST: ...Please.

SCROOGE: ...It's plated.

TWIST: ...I insist.

SCROOGE: Well, all right. (*Takes locket*) What's inside,
a lock of your mummy's hair?

TWIST: I don't know. I've always been too weak to
open it.

(SCROOGE *opens locket and unfolds "Scrooge Lassos the
Moon" picture supposedly inside.*)

EMILY: What is it, Mr Scrooge?

SCROOGE: It's me. (*He turns around picture*) I gave this to
a woman I loved long ago. (*Turns to* TWIST) Sonny!

TWIST: Mr Bumble told me my father was dead.

SCROOGE: He said the same of my child. He kept you
from me so he would be heir to my fortune. The
miserable sloth.

TWIST: Fortune?

SCROOGE: That's right, lad.

TWIST: Daddy! (*He hugs* SCROOGE.)

CRATCHIT: We are childless again, dear.

EMILY: I'll adjust.

(*A knock at the door.* CRATCHIT *opens the door. It is* ANNIE
*in a full-length hooded cloak with her head down, carrying a
cane.*)

CRATCHIT: A poor, blind beggar come to our door
on Christmas Day. We don't have much, but you're
welcome to what we have.

TWIST: Don't give him the goose.

ANNIE: I don't want nothin'. I come to apologize
for liftin' your things.

CRATCHIT: What things?

TWIST: You can say that again.

ANNIE: Your gloves with no fingers, your purse,
a locket, some dust.

TWIST: Annie?

ANNIE: Please don't call the constable. Mr Fagin has
already punished me. (*She removes cloak to reveal big
white pupilless eyes.*)

SCROOGE, TWIST, CRATCHIT & EMILY: Eeewwww!

ANNIE: I've run away and I'm going to be a good
orphan from now on.

CRATCHIT: (*To* EMILY) Dear! Your Christmas wish!

EMILY: Oh no, Bob.

CRATCHIT: You wished for a daughter instead of a son.
And here she is! How would you like to live with us,
Annie?

ANNIE: Leapin' Lords of Parliament. That would be...
a step up from the gutter, I guess.

CRATCHIT: Then it's settled.

TWIST: Daddy Scrooge, tell us a story.

(*A knock at the door. All but* CRATCHIT *take chairs and sit.*
SCROOGE *starts telling story in silence.*)

CRATCHIT: My goodness! We've got more visitors than
the alley behind the Pig 'n' Whistle.

(*Opens door.* FAGIN *and* BUMBLE *stand there, disguised in
scarves.*)

CRATCHIT: Merry Christmas, my friends. How may I be of service?

BUMBLE: We are nomads, traversing with frost-kissed appendages the cobbled byways of this province, and we seek holiday respite in the crackling tongues of an emberous conflagration.

CRATCHIT: I'm somewhat illiterate. You'll have to tone it down a mite.

FAGIN: *(Stepping forward)* We needs to warm our feet by your fire.

CRATCHIT: But of course. Come in and remove your cloaks and scarves.

BUMBLE: *(Putting his hand on his scarf)* Oh no, no. We could not.

FAGIN: We has allergies.

CRATCHIT: Well, the fire is over there.

BUMBLE: I am as grateful as a dolphin given a fish....

(FAGIN *grabs him by the scarf and yanks him to the fireplace.)*

EMILY: Bob, Mr Scrooge is bored. He wants to play truth or dare.

CRATCHIT: Oh, we mustn't. He might find out who put the boric acid in his snuff box.

EMILY: Then you best talk him out of it.

CRATCHIT: I shall. I can't imagine his dares. His ordinary requests have always been nasty enough.

BUMBLE: *(To* FAGIN*)* You cheat! The boy is alive.

FAGIN: Barely. But Scrooge is our concern now. So, what elaborate plan of attack have you choreographed?

BUMBLE: I grab, you stab.

FAGIN: Ingenious.

SCROOGE: So then I took her up to the hayloft and you know the rest. Okay, my turn. Cratchit, did you put the boric acid in my snuff box?

CRATCHIT: Heaven forgive us, we're forgetting about our guests. Let us play something that everyone can enjoy.

SCROOGE: Spin the bottle?

(They all look at EMILY. *She looks around.)*

EMILY: *(Pleadingly)* Bob?

ANNIE: 'Ow about strip whist?

CRATCHIT: A rousing game of blindman's buff!

TWIST: I'm going to kill myself.

CRATCHIT: Where is my kerchief? Oh, I know. *(Takes* FAGIN's *scarf)* This will make a wonderful blindfold. *(Goes to tie it on himself)* Where are my manners? Mr Scrooge, you're the guest of honor. You be the blindman.

(Ties blindfold on SCROOGE. FAGIN *and* BUMBLE *look at each other.)*

FAGIN: I must be dreaming.

SCROOGE: Everybody run.

*(*FAGIN *brandishes knife and comes after* SCROOGE. *All but* ANNIE *scream and run.* ANNIE *runs about aimlessly.)*

SCROOGE: Hee, hee. Here I come.

*(*SCROOGE *moves just as* FAGIN *lunges after him with knife.* FAGIN *misses, and he and* BUMBLE *continue to chase* SCROOGE *as he chases everyone else, who want to stay as far away from him as possible.)*

SCROOGE: Ooo, I love the thrill of the hunt.

*(*FAGIN *and* BUMBLE *surround* SCROOGE.)*

TWIST: Daddy Scrooge. Look out! Behind you!

(FAGIN *spins toward* TWIST *and* SCROOGE *tags him and throws blindfold around his head.*)

SCROOGE: I caught the smelly stranger. You're it.

(FAGIN *takes a mad, blind stab at* SCROOGE *and stabs the goose on the table instead. He rips off the blindfold.* FAGIN, SCROOGE *and* BUMBLE *move close together facing upstage and all grab the knife and try to yank it out of the goose where it is stuck. After three tugs the knife comes out, stabbing one of them. They all spin to face the audience holding their stomachs.* SCROOGE *and* FAGIN *look down. They are fine.* BUMBLE *looks down, sees he is stabbed and immediately falls.* SCROOGE *catches him and lowers him to the ground.*)

BUMBLE: Ohh! I am sailing toward the Stygian shore. My belly bleeds red like a rain-soaked kilt.

SCROOGE: Nephew?

BUMBLE: I must tell you something, uncle.

SCROOGE: Yes.

BUMBLE: Cratchit put the boric acid in your snuff. (*He dies.*)

TWIST: Mr Fagin, you've killed him!

ANNIE: Mr Fagin's here?! (*She's standing right next to him. She then wanders across the room, several feet behind him.*)

SCROOGE: I'm getting the constable, you murderous cretin. And you can expect to be visited by a few ghosts tonight as well.   .

FAGIN: Merry Christmas, Mr Scrooge. (*Lunges at* SCROOGE, *but when he brings his arm down to stab* SCROOGE, *there is no knife.*) What the...?

ANNIE: (*Holding up knife*) Looking for this, Mr Fagin?

FAGIN: Give me that...

(He runs toward her, but TWIST *holds out his crutch and trips him and as he stumbles,* SCROOGE *grabs the goose off the table and stuffs it over* FAGIN's *head.* CRATCHIT *picks up* FAGIN's *scarf that has fallen to the floor, as* FAGIN *continues to thrash around with the goose on his head.)*

CRATCHIT: Okay, Annie, you be it now. *(He ties scarf around her head.)* Can you see anything?

ANNIE: *(Sarcastic)* No.

CRATCHIT: Are you sure?

(He runs, EMILY *squeals with glee,* ANNIE *heads toward* SCROOGE; *she's still brandishing the knife.)*

SCROOGE: She's got a knife!

TWIST: *(Out)* God help us, everyone.

END OF PLAY

PROPERTY LIST

Wooden gruel bowl
FAGIN's box filled with coins and jewels
Crutch
Small wooden stool
Pound note
Bag of coins
Pocket knife
Handkerchief
Pocket watches
Locket
Boxer shorts
Two quill pens
Basket
Pieces of coal
Letters with envleopes
Tin collection box
Jeweled necklaces
Blindfold
Fork
Candle holder, matches and candles
Framed picture of *Scrooge Lassos the Moon*
(gift-wrapped)
Folded picture of *Scrooge Lassos the Moon*
Bucket for punch
Bottle of wine and wine glass
Cigarette
Pudding
Two china tea cups with spoons
Small wooden box or crate
Shovel
Bag of rags
Soft prop goose with large body cavity opening
Two identical prop knives